*Praise for*

# A Visual Journey to ALASKA

"Andrew King has traveled on many cruise vacations. His depictions in this book are essential for anyone seeking more detailed travel information on Alaska. Andrew's stunning photographs serve as visual aids for any traveler who may be undecided on which itineraries to include in their Alaska cruise adventures. I recommend this book as a useful travel guide."

**MaryAnne McRobbie**
Cruise & Vacation Consultant

"I met Andrew King in 2011 when he enrolled in the Personalized Alternative Education program with me at Dr. G.W. Williams Secondary School in Aurora, Ontario. He came to me with such high levels of anxiety about school and academics that he often needed me to walk with him from the parking lot into the building. That first year had its ups and downs for Andrew, but in the end, he surpassed our expectations and earned his credits. In fact, it was my honour to present Andrew with the Most I mproved Student award from our department. The following year, Andrew moved into the regular program to complete his requirements for graduation. I still remember Andrew stopping by to let me know how classes were going, to have me proofread a paper, or to simply catch up on life. It was amazing to see the changes that took place in Andrew, and it was inspiring to watch the growth of his confidence and self-esteem. Andrew had plans for his future, and his determination and hard work set those plans into motion. I was so proud watching Andrew cross the stage at his graduation, and even more thrilled when he was presented with the Character Award for Responsibility, which commemorated his accomplishments. Andrew attended college in Toronto where he studied travel and tourism, then moved to British Columbia to pursue a degree in hospitality. Since then, he has travelled the world on his own and has now written his first book. Andrew is a true inspiration and a testament to what perseverance and dedication can accomplish; he is proof that anything is possible. Congratulations on all you have accomplished, Andrew. I look forward to seeing what the future holds for you."

**Anne Boyne**

"This book has been a labour of love for Andrew. He has combined his love of cruising with his passion for photography, resulting in a delightful glimpse into the wonderful scenery of Alaska. Despite his young age, Andrew has become quite the expert on cruising, ticking off more countries in a few short years than most of us could in a lifetime. Every trip he's taken has been an opportunity for Andrew to hone his photography skills and learn everything there is to know about travelling on cruise ships. Anything Andrew *doesn't* know about cruising probably isn't very important anyway. He has made many friends on his travels and will soon be known as Mr. Cruise! He might even become as famous as the other Mr. Cruise (the one known for his action films)."

**Jacqui Maclaren**

"We thoroughly enjoyed this cruise to Alaska. Andrew's photographs are spectacular, and you feel as if you're actually standing in the places that he describes. His love for his experiences shines through on every page. Andrew's suggestions for where to begin your cruise (ports) are top notch. He also talks about his favorite places to stay and where to eat. I have to say, his restaurant suggestions made our mouths water. This is a delightful travel guide for anyone wanting to experience Alaska from the sea. As he says in the beginning of the book, reading about a place doesn't compare to actually exploring it—but Andrew has done an excellent job presenting it here for us. We see a travel career in his future."

### Renata Natale & T. Lawrence
International Bestselling Authors – *Casting Away: Adventures of A Dead Man*

"*A Visual Journey to Alaska* is a STUNNING BOOK! When I first saw the photographs, I was mesmerized by the colours and detail. Looking from behind the lens and understanding Andrew's love for travel inspires me to want to visit more places. I look forward to seeing what other books Andrew has on the horizon. At a very young age this gentleman has already experienced the magic of many different lands. You will be immersed in a visual cacophony that will have you mesmerized for days. I highly recommend this book."

### Judy O'Beirn
Founder and President of Hasmark Publishing International
International Bestselling Author – *Unwavering Strength Series*

"Andrew King is a remarkable student of the world. His claim that travel has taught him more than sitting in the classroom is validated in his book, *A Visual Journey to Alaska*. As a teacher with an M.Ed. in international teaching, I can absolutely see how this book will inspire a plethora of students from around the world. Andrew's photography skills are immaculate, and he captures some truly stunning visuals of mother nature's grandeur. A must-have for every avid traveler who dreams of cruising the seas. Andrew's pictures truly resonate freedom, creativity, and legacy. I can't wait to see what other books this author has in store for us."

### Pashmina P.
International Bestselling Author – *The Cappuccino Chronicles Trilogy* and *What is A Gupsey?*
M.Ed. International Teaching, Framingham State University

"I am delighted and proud to learn that Andrew King is having a book published! Andrew attended Aurora Montessori School for his Elementary and Middle School education. It was an honor to watch Andrew develop intellectually, physically and emotionally. He was a fine young gentleman with a kind disposition and polite demeanor, always doing his best in his academic and physical development. Socially, Andrew was a peace keeper, always kind and considerate of his fellow students and teachers. He was an honest, hardworking student. He demonstrated an artistic enjoyment and ability, even as a young student. He has carried this artistic ability on to his adult years. It is no surprise to me that Andrew has successfully produced books relating to his travel adventures. Even as a young Middle School student he demonstrated a love and great curiosity for history and our world. Each year after school holidays he regaled the teachers and students with stories of his adventures to exotic locations. Now, as an adult, he shares his in depth knowledge with the world."

### Brenda Glashan
Principal, Aurora Montessori School (2000 – 2015)

# A Visual Journey to

# Alaska

## CRUISING ALASKA

## Andrew King

Hasmark
PUBLISHING
INTERNATIONAL

Published by
Hasmark Publishing
www.hasmarkpublishing.com

Permission should be addressed in writing to bballtime@rogers.com

Editor: Brad Green
brad@hasmarkpublishing.com

Cover & Book Design: Anne Karklins
anne@hasmarkpublishing.com

ISBN 13: 978-1-77482-151-0
ISBN 10: 1774821516

Hasmark
PUBLISHING
INTERNATIONAL

# Acknowledgements

I would like to acknowledge my parents and family for supporting me on all these journeys around the world, and for supporting me on the journey of writing this book.

I would like to acknowledge my amazing team at Hasmark Publishing for bringing this book to fruition. Creating a book for people to see the places I have travelled and experience them through my eyes is a dream come true.

I would like to especially acknowledge my high school teacher, Anne Boyne, for helping me become the person I am, a once struggling student who is now a published author. I credit Anne with helping me find the strong person within—a person who can succeed at anything, and who can become a true inspiration to others.

Finally, I would like to acknowledge my good family friend, MaryAnne McRobbie. Thanks for helping me pick and book these amazing journeys and trips of a lifetime, and for having me join their family on one of my favourite trips ever.

# My Reason for Writing This Book

I'm writing this book because I have done several cruises with my family to Alaska. I have experienced so many new things, many of which I found very enjoyable, and I wanted to share these experiences along with my top suggestions for various cruise ports of Alaska.

I would really like to thank my parents for letting me have these experiences of cruising with them to Alaska, and for letting me see parts of the country that I never thought I would get a chance to see. I appreciate them so much for letting me explore Alaska.

I would like to share a quote—a quote from myself: "You learn more by actually exploring the world than you do by sitting in a classroom learning about it."

# Table of Contents

## Part One: Destination Ports

## Part Two: Departure Ports

# PART ONE:

## Destination Ports

These destinations are some of my recommended
ports for cruises to Alaska and Canada.
They are full of great things to see and do during your visit.

KETCHIKAN, ALASKA

# Ketchikan, Alaska

One of my first memories of cruising to Alaska was sailing into the port of Ketchikan. Ketchikan is a great little town in Alaska. One of the first things I would suggest is stopping in Tongass Trading Company for a souvenir that shows that you visited Ketchikan.

I know most of you are probably asking, *what are some of the best activities to do while in Ketchikan?* One of my top three choices would have to be the Deadliest Catch tour. This tour has so many great things that you don't want to miss including some scenic spots which are visible while sailing out of Ketchikan harbor.

Once you are out of the harbor, they will take you to one of the best areas to see bald eagles in that part of Alaska. When they say this is one of the best places to see bald eagles, they don't lie.

*One of my photos of a bald eagle.*

*Alaskan king crab.*

*My mom holding a snow crab.*

When finished viewing bald eagles, it's on to crab fishing. They show you how they catch different kinds of crab including snow crab, Dungeness crab, and of course, Alaskan king crab.

There are a few other surprises along the way, but I will leave those for you to experience for yourself. One of the things you can't miss is buying a souvenir from the ship itself. I recommend the hoodies; they are really warm and have the vessel name on the back. I have one myself and its perfect for the weather in Alaska.

*The ship that takes you on your crab adventure.*

**My second top choice** is for all you dog lovers out there. You can watch dog sledding on the hills (not on glaciers like you can in other cities). First, you arrive at the dog camp up in the hills. Once you get there, you will be shown around the camp. You can also enjoy some nice views while you're there.

*The amazing waterfall that runs near the camp. They say it looks a lot better when it rains, and the waterfall is flowing.*

Next, they take you to a tent where you can see the equipment used when the dogs run the Iditarod race. You can see what the camp looks like when the racers arrive at the checkpoints. You can also see the bags they carry and some of the winter clothes they wear during the race.

*The bags they use at each checkpoint and clothing worn during the Iditarod race.*

Now comes the real fun. This is what makes the excursion really worth it for anyone, no matter the age. They load you into carts that will be pulled by a team of dogs.

*The team of dogs and a cart, and the track you go on.*

The dog teams pull the carts from the starting point and take you on a short course that was built there. The track isn't very long, but it's enough to show how they use commands from start to finish to get the dogs around the track.

Then, to top it all off, they take you to a little area where they raise puppies that might one day be part of the teams. These puppies may one day become strong like their counterparts and be part of a champion team.

*One of the pups. My mom holding one of the pups.*

**My third top option** is for anyone who likes sports or hard work during an outing—I'm talking about kayaking. This is a very good option for seeing things you can't see from a cruise ship. It's better because you can see things up close and personal. This is perfect for couples or friends who like to spend time doing things together while experiencing new areas and learning new things along the way.

This activity starts out by first learning some kayak safety rules and setting up groups of two. The kayaks are built for two people.

After you and your partner get into the kayak, the adventure begins. You start with a nice paddle down the waterway to view several different scenic spots. At one point, they take you to an area where you can see some of the life that lives on the rocks and on the sides of the little cliffs. For example: a starfish that smells like garlic. This is really something you can't miss out on.

Overall, the three of these options are very good choices for things to do while in Ketchikan. Of course, if your pleasure is shopping or enjoying a nice meal, there are plenty of options in town. All I can say is open your mind while exploring these great areas.

*Colorful kayaks and the kayak loading area.*

*People grouped together for the kayak trip.*

*My mom with the kayaking guides.*

JUNEAU, ALASKA

# Juneau, Alaska

The capital of Alaska is a very nice city to visit on a cruise. There are lots of great things to see, especially nature and the beautiful landscape.

Here, I will share my top two Juneau excursions.

The first excursion I will be talking about is flying in a seaplane over the glaciers and viewing Juneau from the air. What a sight to see! This is a can't-miss experience for flying fanatics and photographers alike.

First, you walk from the ship to the seaplane port area. Next, they will split you up into groups of eight to ten people before walking you down a steep incline to arrive at the loading area for the planes.

*Example of a seaplane.*

After you load into the seaplane is when the fun starts.

*Cockpit of the seaplane.*

Once you take off from the port harbor, they take you to see several breathtaking scenic areas. This is where you photographers will really enjoy the views and get some amazing pictures of glaciers and glacier fields.

*Pictures that I took during the seaplane excursion.*

*Pictures that I took during the seaplane excursion.*

After all the fun in the seaplane, you can walk back to the ship or stay in town to look around or enjoy a nice meal. You can also search for that perfect souvenir in one of many shops.

The second top excursion is a sightseeing tour to Mendenhall Glacier and other scenic areas to get a good view of Juneau.

This tour starts out on a bus heading to some of the scenic areas, one of which is a good view of the harbor of Juneau.

From there, you go on to one of the highest points of Juneau. They take you up in a 4x4 vehicle, and this is where you get a good view of Juneau airport and a few other sights.

*The view of Juneau and the airport.*

When they bring you back down to the bus, it's off to see the beautiful Mendenhall Glacier and visit the park area.

The glacier is the perfect spot to take family pictures or to get some amazing landscape shots of the glacier itself.

These are the best things to do in Juneau. They will make so many memories for you and your family. Juneau is a great place for photographers to add to their portfolios.

# SKAGWAY, ALASKA

# Skagway, Alaska

Skagway is one of the most interesting cruise ports in Alaska with its variety of things to do. While in port, you can take a train up into the mountains, go flying, or see a glacier. But my favorite activity, and the one I want to talk about, is taking a 4x4 Jeep into the mountains and across to the Yukon to a small town called Carcross.

First, you take a bus into the main part of Skagway. This is where all the jeeps and tour guides are waiting for you to join them on the journey.

Here are the things you will need for this journey: First, if you want to drive, you will need a valid driver's license. However, you don't have to drive if you don't want to. You will also need a valid passport to cross the Canadian border. And of course, you need a camera for all the amazing views, snow topped mountains, and other things you will see during this journey.

This journey starts with a drive along the Alaska Highway that leads to Yukon. You will see so many colors in the trees of the hills and other amazing sights.

*The town of Carcross.*

After driving for a while, you will cross the Canadian border into Yukon. It will only take a few minutes for all the jeeps to clear the border and then you are on your way again. Carcross is a very small town, but there are very exciting and scenic things to see.

*A building made to resemble a paddlewheel boat.*

*If you go to this pink building, they will stamp your passport as a keepsake.*

On the way back to the ship, you will stop for photos at the world's smallest desert.

*The world's smallest desert and the jeeps used for the journey.*

# VICTORIA, BRITISH COLUMBIA

# Victoria, British Columbia

Victoria is one of the stops for cruise ships, and is in my home country of Canada. One thing you can do while in Victoria is go to Butchart Gardens for the amazing flowers and to see the butterflies that roam there. But the main attraction in Victoria is whale watching.

Whale watching is an amazing thing to experience. Of course, it's only amazing if you can catch a glimpse of a whale. They take you by bus to a boat that is waiting not far from the cruise ships in Victoria harbor.

*This is how close to your cruise ship you get.*

During my trip there was only one whale, but don't let that turn you away. I have heard from others who have seen many whales while out on this journey.

If you're lucky you might see some Canadian war ships, coast guard helicopters, or an old Canadian war vessel.

*Canadian military ships from different eras.*

*Canadian Coast Guard helicopter.*

# Glacier Cruising

Your Alaskan cruise itinerary may take you to one of two scenic glacier areas: Glacier Bay Park or Tracy Arm fjord, both of which are very beautiful areas to see.

Tracy Arm is a magnificent glacier in its own right, along with everything else you see as you travel down this narrow fjord.

As you get closer, the glacier starts to seem bigger. Sometimes you can see pieces that have broken off.

Once the ship gets as close as possible, the captain will stop and do a full rotation so everyone can get a clear view of the glacier. My tip is to get as far forward on the ship as you can so that you can see the glacier for the longest period of time. This is what I did.

The other large glacier area you can visit on a cruise is Glacier Bay. This is the larger glacier and the most scenic cruising.

You can see two glaciers on the Glacier Bay tour, one of which is bigger and better than the other. If you're lucky, you might get to see some of the glacier fall off. One way to know this is about to happen is hearing a loud cracking sound, almost like the sound of cracking thunder. That's when you know something might happen. Next you have to locate the area of the glacier that is cracking and ready to fall. Again, my advice is to get as close to the front of the ship as possible to get the best view.

# PART TWO:

## *Departure Ports*

The three primary departure points for Alaska cruises
are Seattle, Vancouver, and San Francisco.
I will talk about the larger two, Vancouver and San Francisco.
I will give suggestions about where to stay and what you
can do in these two port cities. I will start with Vancouver,
one of the most beautiful cities in the province of British Columbia
and one of the best cities to set off from for your Alaskan cruise.

# VANCOUVER, BRITISH COLUMBIA

# Vancouver, British Columbia

Here are my top two suggestions for where to stay when starting your cruise from Vancouver. The first is Hotel Fairmont Waterfront, which is the closest to the port. All you have to do is walk across the street and you're right there. One of the best ways to see the ships is to go to the lobby and look out the front windows.

The other hotel I suggest is the Sheraton Wall Centre. This hotel is a bit further from the port, but is very nice overall. It has two towers and tons of rooms and is still an easy walk to the cruise port. It's a bit further of a walk than from Hotel Fairmont Waterfront, but all you need to do is walk straight down Burrard Street to arrive at the port.

Here is a list of some of the best options for things to do in Vancouver:

• Grouse Mountain

• Stanley Park

• Vancouver Aquarium

• Vancouver Lookout

• Olympic Cauldron

*View from the port area with Lions Gate Bridge in the background.*

At Grouse Mountain you can go skiing in the winter, and in the summer months they have hiking and other family activities. After the cable car ride, you can ride the ski lift even higher for a better view.

*View from the ski lift.*

Stanley Park is one of the best areas in all of Vancouver. You can experience the aquarium, but you can also go walking or biking on the seawall. It can take several hours to walk completely around, and a bit less time to bike. You can relax along the way, and there are a couple of beaches on the far side of the seawall to enjoy. There are several places to stop for photos along the way, especially if you want to get a good picture of Lions Gate Bridge.

*Totem poles*

Inside Stanley Park you can see some pretty cool totem poles. They have so many colors and so much great history. They show the work of the Indigenous people of Canada.

Vancouver Lookout is one of the other great areas to get a good view of the harbor, and another great photo opportunity. You can get some great landscape photos of the mountain range in Vancouver.

The lookout is a great way to experience Vancouver and see large portions of the city.

One of the other great sights to see is the Olympic Cauldron—the location of the flame from the 2010 Winter Olympics. The cauldron is located right at the harbourfront, just down the street from the cruise port. It's well worth the visit to see a piece of Canadian Olympic history.

The next thing I will share with you is a list of the best places to go get something to eat in Vancouver. These places are my recommendations, but of course there are other places to eat depending on what type of food you want.

*View from Vancouver Lookout*

Here are my personal picks for places to eat while staying in the city of Vancouver:

- Earls Kitchen + Bar
- Cardero's
- White Spot
- Bellagio Café

All these places I have listed are the best food experiences and the best food overall. You can't miss any of these during your stay in Vancouver. You don't know what you are missing.

Overall, my best advice if you are taking a cruise from Vancouver is to give yourself a few days to explore and experience what the city has to offer.

*The Olympic Cauldron*

*View of Lions Gate Bridge*

SAN FRANCISCO, CALIFORNIA

# San Francisco, California

The other primary departure point for Alaskan cruises is San Francisco—the *Golden Gate City*.

San Francisco is one of my personal top choices for travel, even if it's not for a cruise. I like San Francisco because of the many things to do and see while visiting or while taking some time before a cruise.

Let's start with the best place to stay while in San Francisco. Fisherman's Wharf Marriott is one of the best places to stay because it's so close to food and shopping, and because it is also very close to the cruise port. This hotel is a really nice and relaxing place to be.

Now, let's focus on some of the great food establishments nearby the hotel. You can get tons of great food and small snacks at a place called Boudin Bakery. They have a lot of great food, and my favorite is soup in a bread bowl. You can watch the staff create bread art in the shape of bears and alligators and other creatures. You must stop there on any trip to San Francisco.

The best place to get breakfast and snacks and fruit during the right season is Pier 39. My advice is to get a crepe. My personal picks would be Nutella or chocolate with marshmallow—both are amazing. Of course, they do have meat and vegetable crepes as well, and some other good breakfast options.

The other great advantage of Pier 39 is all the snack foods like mini doughnuts or chocolate chip cookies. Another great thing to get while at Pier 39 is pizza. There is a great place there where the pizza is perfect in every possible way. And of course, the other popular restaurant at Pier 39 is Bubba Gump Shrimp Company—the restaurant named after the movie *Forrest Gump*. Here, they will actually ask you questions about the movie.

The biggest attraction at Pier 39 are the sea lions. As soon as you arrive at Pier 39, you will hear them. You will be wondering what the sound is. It is the sound of sea lions play fighting or behaving in their own way. The biggest myth among locals is that if the sea lions are gone from the pier it's because they can sense an earthquake coming. This is one of the biggest myths in San Francisco.

Now, let's talk about the other big tourist spots in San Francisco. The first one is Alcatraz—aka "The Rock"—which is an island in the middle of San Francisco Bay. The thing people enjoy about Alcatraz are the prison tours. They offer two different options, a day tour and a night tour. During the tour, you are provided with an audio headset so that you can hear stories of the past as you view the famous cells of prisoners who attempted to escape. I know one of the prison escape stories is true because the History Channel did a story about it and provided quite compelling evidence. The night tour is the same, but when it's dark you get a better feeling of what it was probably like for the prisoners that went through Alcatraz.

The next tourist site I will talk about is, of course, the thing that gave San Francisco its nickname: the Golden Gate Bridge. This is a true can't-miss for anyone visiting the city. There are a few cool ways to experience the bridge. You can bike or walk across it, but what I consider the best way to see the bridge is by tour boat. There are a few local tour companies that will sail you right under the bridge. Of course, let's hope that the day you choose to experience the Golden Gate Bridge has clear weather. The weather can be very tricky, and a lot of the time the bridge is covered by fog. Personally, I suggest days with good weather. My other suggestion for experiencing the bridge is by taking an open-top tour bus. There is a company or two that offer driving tours across the bridge. These tours provide a good vantage point for seeing the city from the other side of the bay. It's also a cool way to see Alcatraz from a distance. Always remember to take your camera with you to get great photos for the family, or to just get good photos for remembering the trip.

The Golden Gate Bridge is a marvel in itself, and one of the many reasons people travel to San Francisco. The reasons I love going to San Francisco are the Golden Gate Bridge, the many other scenic areas to take great photos and make family memories, and all the great food.

This photo was taken on the San Francisco side looking towards the other side of the bridge. As you can see, the weather was perfect. This is one of the very few times I have been to San Francisco and seen it this clear. It is a perfect memory.

The next great place to visit in San Francisco is Coit Tower, the highest point in the city. If you are up for some serious cardio, walking to the top tower is a real workout.

The other great advantage of being up Coit Tower is the view of San Francisco Bay. It's the perfect place to enjoy seeing the city from high up, and the perfect opportunity to get another great photo.

The city has many famous places to stop, including Lombard Street—the most crooked street in San Francisco. A lot of people drive their cars down the winding street just to say they did it. It's quite a thing to see. I won't ruin the surprise for you with a photo because you might not believe your eyes. It's something you need to see for yourself in person.

And finally, the best for last. If you have a real sweet tooth while in San Francisco, you need to visit the original Ghirardelli Ice Cream & Chocolate Shop at Ghirardelli Square. This is another can't-miss if you really want to have the best experience. I suggest having a really light dinner before heading to

Ghirardelli's. One of my favorites is the brownie; it's so soft and chewy with a lot of chocolate infused in it. But of course, if you really want to go heavy, you can get an ice cream sundae with three or four scoops of ice cream, chocolate sauce, and tons of whipped cream, finished off with a cherry on top.

The last thing I will suggest for San Francisco is to take your time and enjoy the amazing sights. There are many filming locations you can visit and different parts of the town to see. I highly recommend taking a trip to San Francisco, or a cruise departing from the Golden Gate City.

I hope you have fun on your trip to Alaska,
and hopefully you can use my ideas to make it that much more memorable.
Enjoy your trip to the fullest!

For more information about the author, please visit:

**Instagram @cruisepicsbykinger**


**More books on the horizon!**

# About the Author

Andrew King is from Ontario, Canada. The first thing you need to know about this book and the author behind it is that he has been travelling for years and developed his passion for travel at a young age.

Andrew believes that the greatest thing about travelling is being able to experience new countries and new parts of the world all while seeing things you have never seen before. Andrew classifies his many trips across the world to Alaska, the Caribbean, Europe, Australia and New Zealand as some of his greatest journeys. In this book Andrew hopes to take readers along with him and to pass on his knowledge to other travellers so that they can take their own journeys.

With every donation, a voice will be given to
the creativity that lies within the hearts of
our children living with diverse challenges.

By making this difference, children that may
not have been given the opportunity to have their
Heart Heard will have the freedom to create
beautiful works of art and musical creations.

*Donate by visiting*

**HeartstobeHeard.com**

We thank you.

Printed in the USA
CPSIA information can be obtained
at www.ICGtesting.com
LVHW061051261123
764950LV00014B/57